★★★ M109A6 PALADINS

BY CARLOS ALVAREZ

BELLWETHER MEDIA · MINNEAPOLIS, MN

Are you ready to take it to the extreme?
Torque books thrust you into the action-packed
world of sports, vehicles, and adventure. These books
may include dirt, smoke, fire, and dangerous stunts.
WARNING: read at your own risk.

Library of Congress Cataloging-in-Publication Data

Alvarez, Carlos, 1968-
  M109A6 Paladins / by Carlos Alvarez.
      p. cm. – (Torque: military machines)
  Summary: "Amazing photography accompanies engaging information about M109A6 Paladins.
The combination of high-interest subject matter and light text is intended for students in grades 3
through 7"–Provided by publisher.
  Includes bibliographical references and index.
  ISBN 978-1-60014-283-3 (hardcover : alk. paper)
  1. M109 Paladin (Howitzer)–Juvenile literature. I. Title.
  UF652.A45 2010
  623.4'2–dc22

                                        2009008488

This edition first published in 2010 by Bellwether Media, Inc.

The photographs in this book are reproduced through the courtesy of the United States Department of
Defense.

Printed in the United States of America.

CONTENTS

THE M109A6 IN ACTION

The sound of gunfire echoes over the desert. United States Army troops are battling a heavily-armored enemy. An M109A6 Paladin rumbles over the sand. It is there to help the U.S. troops. Its **tracked wheels** give it good grip on the rough ground.

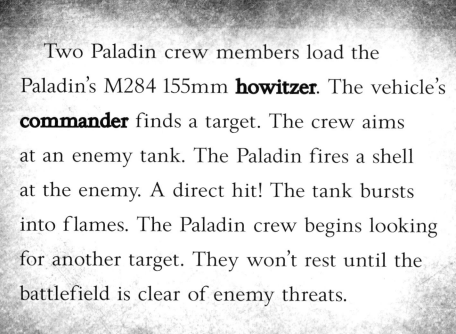

Two Paladin crew members load the Paladin's M284 155mm **howitzer**. The vehicle's **commander** finds a target. The crew aims at an enemy tank. The Paladin fires a shell at the enemy. A direct hit! The tank bursts into flames. The Paladin crew begins looking for another target. They won't rest until the battlefield is clear of enemy threats.

SELF-PROPELLED HOWITZER

The M109A6 Paladin is a self-propelled howitzer. It is set on a system of tracked wheels. It is similar to a tank. It supports U.S. Army troops in ground combat.

The Paladin is the "A6" model of the M109. The Army has used some version of the M109 since 1963. The Paladin model first entered service in 1991. The Army will begin replacing the Paladin in 2014. The new self-propelled howitzer will be called the XM1203 NLOS-C.

★ ★ ★

★ FAST FACT ★

The Paladin carries 133 gallons of fuel.

WEAPONS
AND FEATURES

★ ★ ★

The main weapon of the Paladin is its M284 155mm howitzer. It can fire huge rounds as far as 15 miles (24 kilometers). It can fire rocket-powered rounds even further. The M284 has a semi-automatic loading system. This allows it to fire up to four shots per minute.

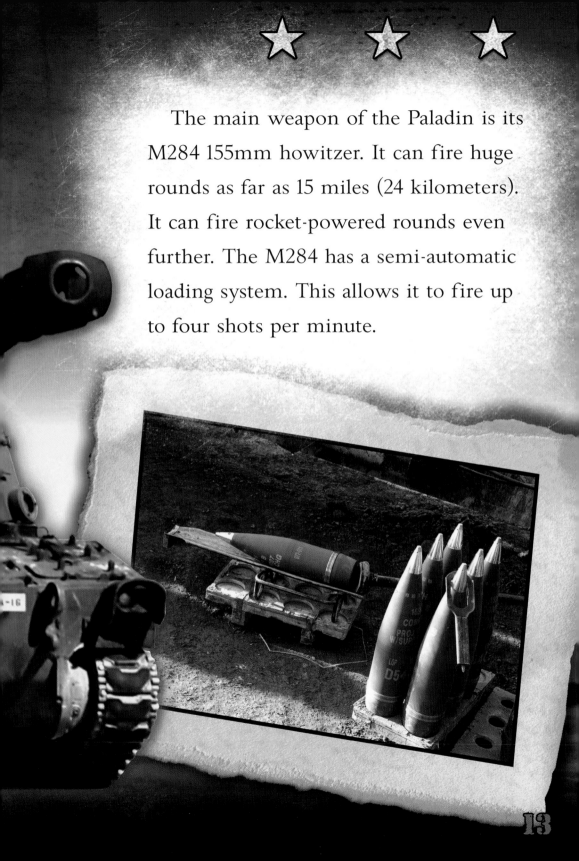

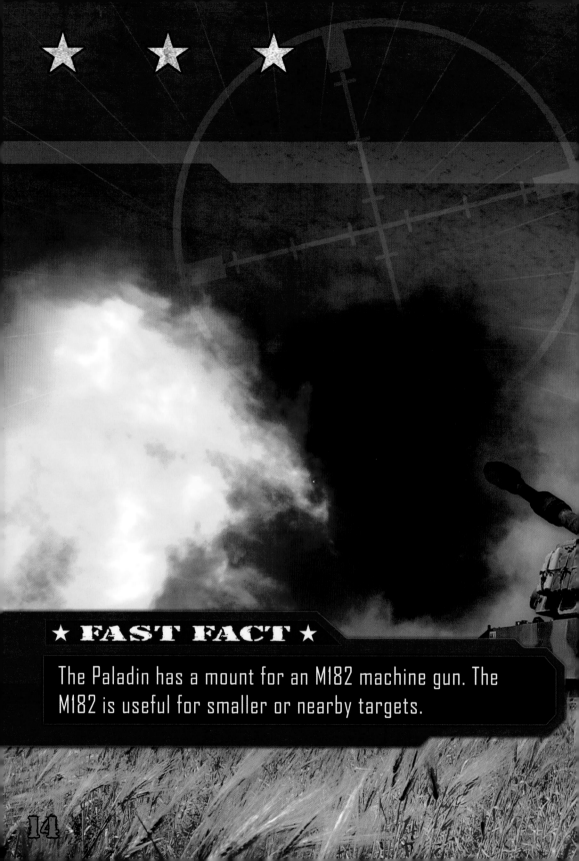

★ ★ ★

★ FAST FACT ★

The Paladin has a mount for an M182 machine gun. The M182 is useful for smaller or nearby targets.

The Paladin needs more than firepower to succeed. It has a powerful 440 **horsepower** engine. This engine can push a Paladin up to 40 miles (65 kilometers) per hour. It also has strong **Kevlar** armor. The armor protects the crew from enemy fire.

Paladins have other gear to help them on **missions**. **Night-vision goggles** help the Paladin driver see at night. Communications gear lets a Paladin crew talk securely with others. They talk with other Paladins and superior officers. Some Paladins have additional weapons to help them on their missions. One such weapon is a **grenade launcher**.

M109A6 SPECIFICATIONS:

Primary Function: Self-propelled howitzer

Length: 30 feet (9.1 meters)

Height: 10.7 feet (3.3 meters)

Width: 10.3 feet (3.1 meters)

Weight: 56,400 pounds (25,600 kilograms)

Speed: 40 miles (64 kilometers) per hour

Engines: 440 horsepower, two-cycle diesel

Range: 214 miles (344 kilometers)

M109A6 MISSIONS

The Paladin's main mission is to support ground troops. It is highly mobile. It can move to get within firing range of enemy targets. Its powerful howitzer can take out heavily armored targets. It can also destroy fortified enemy positions.

The Paladin has "shoot and scoot" capability. It can stop, aim, shoot, and be on the move again in less than one minute.

Four crew members operate a Paladin. The commander is in charge of the mission. The driver steers the Paladin into position. The loader and gunner work together. They load and fire the howitzer. Paladins often work together in groups. They coordinate their attacks to best support the troops on the ground.

GLOSSARY

commander—the crew member in charge of a Paladin

grenade launcher—a weapon that fires small explosives called grenades

horsepower—a unit for measuring the power of an engine

howitzer—a type of cannon with a short-length to medium-length barrel

Kevlar—a very strong fiber used to make items such as bulletproof vests and armor

mission—a military task

night-vision goggles—a special set of glasses that allow the wearer to see at night

tracked wheels—a set of wheels surrounded by a tough, flexible track; the track gives a vehicle, such as a Paladin or a tank, excellent grip on almost any surface.

TO LEARN MORE

AT THE LIBRARY

Baker, David. *M109 Paladin.* Vero Beach, Fla.: Rourke, 2007.

David, Jack. *United States Army.* Minneapolis, Minn.: Bellwether, 2008.

Parker, Steve. *The M109A6 Paladin.* Mankato, Minn.: Capstone, 2008.

ON THE WEB

Learning more about military machines is as easy as 1, 2, 3.

1. Go to www.factsurfer.com.

2. Enter "military machines" into search box.

3. Click the "Surf" button and you will see a list of related Web sites.

With factsurfer.com, finding more information is just a click away.

INDEX